Lucy

Sarah

Alfie

Olivia

Can you find Tom and Millie's friends in the book?

Ruby

Harry

Toby

Dylan

Poppy

Florence

Clive

For Bella

ORCHARD BOOKS
338 Euston Road, London NW1 3BH

Orchard Books Australia
Level 17/207 Kent Street, Sydney, NSW 2000

First published in 2012 by Orchard Books

ISBN 978 1 40831 176 9

Text and illustrations © Guy Parker-Rees 2012

The right of Guy Parker-Rees to be identified as the author
and illustrator of this book has been asserted by him in accordance with
the Copyright, Designs and Patents Act, 1988.

A CIP catalogue record for this book is available from the British Library.

1 3 5 7 9 10 8 6 4 2

Printed in China

Orchard Books is a division of Hachette Children's Books,
an Hachette UK company.
www.hachette.co.uk

Tom & Millie's
GREAT
BIG
TREASURE HUNT

Guy Parker-Rees

What can you see
on every busy page?

ORCHARD

Tom and Millie are excited they're going on a great, big treasure hunt! They have a list of Very Important Things to find.

"Quick!" says Tom. "The list says the treasure hunt starts at the beach and the first clue is on a square red flag."
"Let's go!" says Millie.

There's so much to see at
the beach! Their friend Adam is licking
a pink ice cream, Jake is wearing his red cap
and Hannah is floating in her yellow ring.
"Look, Tom!" calls Millie. "There's a square
red flag on Matt's sandcastle . . .

". . . and I've found the next clue! It's on the red flag."
"What are you two doing?" asks Matt. "Can I help?"
"Come along!" says Tom. "We're collecting these
Very Important Things."

Playground
2 Round Blue
Tambourines

"I love treasure hunts,"
says Matt. "Let's go!"
So Tom, Millie and Matt set
off for the playground.

At the playground, they see
Sophie cuddling two teddy bears,
Max pushing two yellow diggers
and Arthur wearing a purple
t-shirt with two orange triangles on it.
"Listen! I can hear music," says Millie.

"It's Sarah, shaking two round blue tambourines!" says Tom.

"Now we have one red flag and two blue
tambourines," says Millie.
"And look, here's our next clue,
on one of the tambourines," adds Tom.

"Come with us, Sarah," says Matt.
"We're on a treasure hunt!"
"I love finding things," says Sarah. "Let's go!"
So Tom, Millie, Matt and Sarah set off for town.

In town, they see Sam holding
three yellow balloons, Noah riding
his tricycle with three orange wheels, and Lucy
wearing a dress with three white flowers on it.

"There's Toby outside the Party Shop!" says Tom.
"But where are the three purple triangle hats?"
"There they are," says Sarah, "in the window!"

"Great," says Tom, "now we have one red flag,
two blue tambourines . . ."
" . . . and three purple hats," adds Millie.
"Look, there's the next clue,
on a purple hat!" says Matt.

Play Centre
4 Yellow
Balls

So Tom, Millie, Matt and Sarah
set off for the play centre.
"And me!" says Toby.

At the play centre, they see Dylan making a tower with four blue squares, Olivia balancing on a ball with four green stripes on it and Ruby jumping over four orange triangles.

"I can see lots of coloured balls," says Tom. "And there are four yellow ones next to Freddie's cart!" adds Millie.

"Now we have one red flag, two blue tambourines, three purple hats and four yellow balls," says Millie.
"Where's the next clue?" asks Tom.
"There! On the yellow balls," says Millie.

"I love cake!" says Freddie. "Let's go!"
So Tom, Millie, Matt, Sarah, Toby and Freddie
set off for the market.

At the market, they see Alfie carrying five big brown oval eggs, Harry buying five triangles of yellow cheese, and Poppy, sitting next to her basket with five pink flowers on it.

"There's Florence, at the cake stand," says Millie.
"And I can see the five pink square cakes!" says Tom.

"Now we have everything on the list!" says Tom.
"But what's it all for?" everyone wants to know.
"We'll find out soon," says Millie.
"Here's the last clue, inside a cake box!"

"Come on, everyone,
let's go!"

"It's the Sunnytown Summer Fair!"
say Tom and Millie.
"And look – everything
we collected is here!
Let's all join the fun!"

Find 6 red stars to win this cake!

Sophie

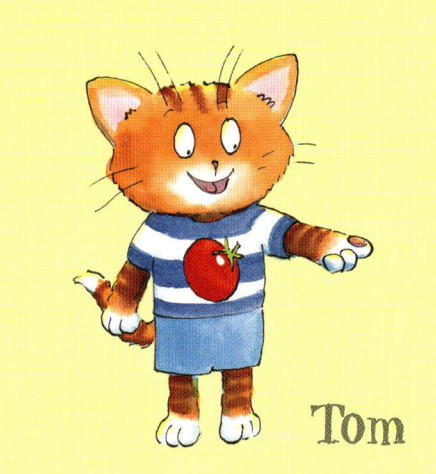

Tom

Adam

Hannah

Freddie

Jake

Max

Millie

Noah

Sam

Matt

Arthur